To my wife Rachel

Life can be accepted or changed. If it is not accepted, it must be changed.
If it cannot be changed it must be accepted.
Winston Churchill

Contents

PREFACE

"Enjoy life... this is not a rehearsal"

Anon

This book is aimed anyone who has a lot to do and little time in which to do it. Whether you work in a company or from home, whether your business is in retail, service provision or construction, if you are a stay-at-home spouse or just retired and spend time reading or pottering around in the garden, this book can help you make the most out of the time you have.

I learnt very early that there are those who live to work, and those who work to live. I most definitely fell and still fall, into the latter category, for as I see things, life is there to be enjoyed and there are no pockets in a shroud.

This book was written nearly 20 years ago when I suddenly felt the urge to put on paper what had been bugging me for many years. A few people read my original manuscript, but I never took it any further.

Now years later I dusted off the original manuscript, figuratively speaking, and gave it a read. I realised that over the years nothing had changed, my original observations and complaints still prevail, and the suggested solutions are in my mind still applicable.

So here is the new version, updated extensively but the message is essentially just as it was. Technology has changed, new laws have been introduced, there are more people in the world but other than that the same old same old.

The essence of the matter is there are still too many people spending far too many hours working, and not achieving anything. The amount of time spent at work does not translate into the output achieved. Those guilty of this absurd practice will deny anything is wrong and will defend to the bitter end the importance of their approach, and complain later.

I spent most of my working life in the Computer Industry, as a programmer, systems analyst, and then progressed through the management ladder. Most of our work was project based, we had to deliver programs, systems and solutions to customers according to strict guidelines and timetables. I realise that not all businesses operate in this way. However, if you think about it, everything we do has time and resource constraints, needs to be done correctly and according to predetermined requirements.

Based on my experience I'm convinced certain people are more prone to working long hours, whilst achieving little. These people display common behaviours and personalities, which I trust, will help you identify (and avoid) them. These observations were gathered over years living in different countries, interacting with a wide range of cultures and working in many different industries.

Of course, by doing so I have inevitably annoyed certain people. I do not apologise for this, nor do I apologise for being slightly less than politically correct. As with so many of the current taboo subjects and forbidden stereotypes, they stemmed purely from general observations of various groups' behaviours, nothing more.

The entire world operates based on general behaviour patterns across the different cultures, ages, colours, sexes, beliefs, sizes and more. Every insurance policy is based on age, sex, where you live, health condition and more. People over the age of 75 are more likely to die in the next 5 years than those aged 30. Younger drivers are more of a hazard than older drivers because that's what years of statistics indicate. And this is because younger drivers have less experience that older ones. This is not judgemental, it's a fact. Women tend to make better mothers than men, pretty obvious really.

I have also used the opportunity of having a dig at some of the practices and trends predominant in today's world. Some of my finger pointing you may feel does not have a direct bearing on the subject on hand; forgive me, but the intention is to ease the tension somewhat and provide further background to the book.

Some years ago, one of my erstwhile managers, when explaining why he felt I was right for the job for which I had applied, said that he thought I was lazy. I was taken aback as I had always been taught that laziness was a vice. He explained that lazy people tend to make sure that they do a task once only, correctly and in the most efficient manner possible. He had made a very valid point and based on that I would accept and live with my laziness.

"Efficiency is intelligent laziness"

David Dunham

We do not have enough time in which to do everything we'd like, and we therefore need to make better use of the time on hand. I have met people who, once they have started a reading a book, feel they must finish it, even if the book holds no interest whatsoever. I would disagree strongly, life is too short to drink box wine, and likewise life is too short to read poor books.

There will of course always be reasons to put in extra effort, chalk up the overtime, and those who succeed will state the success was due to honest hard work. There are many textbooks on all aspects of business and efficiency and all have points which, if understood and applied correctly, will make life easier. I do not intend to pass judgement on any of these practices; what I hope to get across is that, with a few simple guidelines and a distinct change in attitude, you will be able to increase your output, and hence your effectiveness to the organisation for which you work. And you will have the time and the energy to enjoy life to the fullest.

This book is aimed at those who want to succeed and in addition want to have the time to pursue other interests. It is a practical guide to being smarter with your time and getting the most out of life.

You don't want to become an exponent of The Longest Day.

PART ONE – SETTING THE SCENE

"You should never let your fears prevent you from doing what you know is right"

Aung San Suu Kyi

Before I proceed let me introduce you to what we are facing regarding people working such long (and frequently) inefficient hours. The population growth of the world is staggering. In 1900 the population was 1.6 billion, 1960 it was just over 3 billion, 1990 it was 3.3 billion and in 2018 7.6 billion. Technology has grown in leaps and bounds.

The world is getting smaller, the global village is upon us, and this brings a host of new challenges. Where in the past we would wait until the following morning, or the start of a new week to conduct business, we now hop on the Internet at any time of the day or night and do whatever is necessary. Instead of waiting for the TV News Bulletins or daily newspapers for share prices, our phones are updated directly 24 hours a day. With the continued availability of up to date information we are being forced to try to keep abreast of new developments. We must be prepared to read, absorb, assimilate, make decisions and act at a moment's notice. Some feel that the current generation have it easier than in the old days. Whether this is true or not, each generation has to face different challenges and these in turn affect the way they behave. Let's have a look.

---

1 - Introduction

"We live in a moment of history where change is so speeded up that we begin to see the present only when it is already disappearing"

R.D.Laing

This pressure makes it even more important to have that leisure time and enjoy it. This can only be achieved with a healthy balance between earning the money, and spending (enjoying) it.

It is accepted that the older we are the faster time seems to pass us by and possibly the most common excuse for not doing something is 'not enough time'.

Many of you will have had the opportunity of travelling in Europe, around some of the old and very beautiful cities. What strikes one most is the level of detail that is evident in the buildings, structures, paintings and furniture of the yesteryears. There was more time available then, less people and no shortage of opportunities to think, ponder, create and experiment.

Invitations to events and the acceptance thereof were conducted by mail; social gatherings sometimes went on for days rather than hours. Only fifty years ago there was time to take an overseas trip by boat. Nowadays the business traveller arrives at the boarding gate just in time, travels in a suit, arrives the next morning at the destination and immediately rushes off to attend a meeting. Is this really an efficient use of time, remembering that the traveller has had a minimal sleep, no real time to relax, and yet is expected to be bright-eyed and bushy-tailed on arrival? I think not.

When I was growing up, outside interests were encouraged and participation in sport at school was compulsory. Sport was generally amateur, and those participating did so for the love of the game as much as anything. In those days businesses and organisations had hierarchical structures and managers took decisions and made them work. The concept of accepting responsibility for one's actions was understood and accepted, likewise the rewards accrued accordingly and appropriately.

People too have changed over the years. The speed at which we are being forced to live has meant that many individuals have been placed in positions for which they are not properly qualified.

"Time is what we want most ... but what we use worst"

William Penn

How many of you or your friends have time to read anything significant, I'm not talking about the sports page of the local newspaper or the share prices? We are in a 24/7 (twenty-four hours a day, seven days a week) situation where Seven-Eleven (the original long-hours convenience store) is no longer the front-runner of all-hours-availability. With the advent of internet and e-commerce it is possible to buy anything from anywhere and have it delivered to wherever you want it, at the push of a few buttons. One would think that these easier ways of doing things would leave us with more free time, but it doesn't work this way. As information is readily available, success is being determined by how quickly you can react to the information and gain that competitive advantage. So, what do we do, we work longer hours, and this fast becomes a habit and then a *fait accompli?*

We frequently hear people say they don't have time to do something. Probing further you may find that these extraordinarily busy people have already decided what they want to do, and the 'too busy' is merely an excuse. And they're happy about it. It's true there is insufficient time to do everything you would like to do but if making the choice and living with this is okay, you do not have a problem, yet.

Incidentally have you noticed how these overworked people impose their inevitable inabilities on others around them? Take the highly stressed individual who works till all hours doing something. This person invariably calls meetings outside normal hours, sets ridiculous time frames, and expects other efficient people to give up their own time to help him or her achieve their goals.

Bear in mind there will always be occasions where overtime is required; the art is to treat these as the exceptions, not the rule. Distinguishing between necessary and unnecessary is difficult as the exceptions can quickly become the norm. As a guideline more than a week of continual overtime is too much and becoming a habit. Typically, overtime is required during stock takes, financial period ends, response to tenders and the inevitable 'rush job'. If you are in a service industry, where you are required to maintain customer's equipment, such maintenance may need to be performed after hours to minimise the disruption to the customer. Practicality determines that overtime will never disappear completely, however it can be reduced significantly by awareness and planning.

Some organisations pay their staff overtime which is quite acceptable provided the staff do not abuse this by under-performing during normal hours thus necessitating the extra time. (This happens all the time, trust me!).

There will be many of you who will immediately raise a host of different reasons, some of which may even be valid, as to why what I'm suggesting cannot be achieved. Some of the suggestions may be difficult to put into practice. The main reason is likely to be the attitude of your immediate superior (I've always thought this a silly term, senior in age or status is seldom a definitive definition of superior). More about this later.

Back to The Longest Day

2 - The Down Side of Long Hours

"Until you value yourself, you won't value your time. Until you value your time, you will not do anything with it"

M. Scott Peck

The proverb from the 17th Century, 'All work and no play makes Jack a dull boy', still holds true. In this chapter I highlight some effects of persistent long hours and the effect this may have not only on you but your friends, family and colleagues as well. Its unhealthy, unproductive and uninspiring.

It has frequently been reported, and supported by scientific observations, that an average person's concentration period is approximately 45 minutes. Or we work continuously for long periods never thinking for a moment that we may not be achieving what we should. Excessive hours you put in seldom result in increased productivity. The information absorption factor is greatly reduced, and errors start creeping in. And what is worse these errors are seldom discovered until much later.

As stated in the beginning the pace of life is considerably higher than it used to be and this results in another all too common ailment called Stress. And this is serious. Your health and therefore that of your family, assuming you still have one by then, is adversely affected.

If you spend all your life in the office, working hard because *'there is no-one else to do it'*, and *'if I want it done right, I must do it myself'*, you will become the proverbial boring pain in the arse. Why, because you are avoiding outside stimuli, you don't read the news, gossip columns, or the sports pages. You have no hobbies, no time to watch, no time to listen, and your world inevitably shrinks.

As you spend all the time at your desk, nose to the grindstone, you cannot help but notice that the others around you, your peers, pop off to the pub after work, go to the gym, meet for supper and a whole host of other leisure activities. After a while, and probably sooner than you think, you will become envious, then jealous and finally downright angry,

'How can you all enjoy yourselves when I'm stuck here working?'

Now you start putting your peers under pressure, and this is both unfair and unnecessary. You will succeed in making a few feel guilty and they may well end up like you, deeply immersed in something and not really understanding why. The others, those enlightened ones, will simply keep out of your way.

The next step in this sequence is that you will ultimately alienate yourself completely from your peers, and your friends. Those very good friends will initially understand your extra effort, and in order to maintain the *status quo*, will continue to ask you out,

'How about lunch, let's go for a run after work?'

However, after a while this too will cease. People can only take rejection for so long.

Your protection mechanism now kicks in, and you will find yourself making excuses for both your own and their behaviour. These old friends of yours are immature, not able to accept the responsibility the job demands, do not understand how successful careers are built, and so on. This will then expand into a feeling of superiority; you're better than they are. There is yet another very serious consequence of this behaviour, especially if you have a boss who thinks like you do and encourages this.

"When a man tells you he got rich through hard work, ask him: Whose?"

Don Marquis

There are health issues related to long hours, it is universally acknowledged that exercise is necessary and ideal way to relax after a long day's work. A tired body allows one to relax, a tired mind tends to keep one up until all hours of the night. I am not saying that the exercise or sport needs to be at the highest level, just being active, participating in individual or team activities is good for the body and soul. Hobbies whatever they may be provide another way to relax by concentrating on something different, totally unrelated to work, thus allowing one to unwind.

In short if you behave like this, say goodbye to your friends, The Longest day owns you.

3 - Why do People do this

"People don't change their behaviour unless it makes a difference for them to do so"

Fran Tarkenton

In this chapter I try to identify the type of person who regularly work long hours and in so doing help you identify them and help them. The 'them' may be you but that is for you to know. I share with you some of my thoughts and observations. You may have opinions but will certainly be able to relate to some of what I say below, even add to the list of the 'long hour' brigade. Let's see what happens.

The real question is why do people insist of working these long hours? Challenge these people and they will initially deny any such habit, and then come up with a million and one excuses for being the way they are. I truly feel that many of these people labour under tremendous misconceptions, for example:

- Productivity is related to hours worked
- People can be indispensable
- I am indispensable
- The customer is always right!

Have you ever tried to broach this subject of long hours, and question why they insist on working excessive overtime? The excuses simply role off the tongue, here are some you may encounter.

'I can't delegate, they're all useless'

This very common response carries little weight and may even indicate that the individual concerned has no confidence in his or her own ability and therefore cannot risk an "underling" showing them up.

'If you want it done properly then do it yourself'

Similar to the above, the person may not have a clue how to do the job and therefore is not in a position to explain it to someone else.

"If you can't explain it simply, you don't understand it well enough"

Albert Einstein

'We do not have enough staff'

There will never be sufficient staff or resources and the success of good business is to make optimal use of your resources. What may be true is that you do not have the right staff, and this is discussed in more detail later.

'The customer needs it now'

and

'The customer comes first'

Whilst there are cases where the customer needs it now, most customers are human and will understand the need for waiting. What customers will however insist on is that if a future date is promised, this date is adhered to.

'I'm a perfectionist'

This is one of my pet hates as I have yet to meet someone who really understands what perfection is and then how to achieve it. I have dedicated more space to this later.

'I'm all confused'

This is the 'last stand' statement, frequently made when all other excuses have been flogged to death or it is realised by the incumbent that any more bulls**t will be treated as such. I have seen this *"I'm confused what should I do"* being extremely successful in gaining sympathy from those lesser-informed individuals, many of whom suffer from the same work-a-holism. The usual result is that the person concerned makes no decisions, runs around being a pain to all who will listen (if this is the boss then you're forced to listen), ultimately achieving absolutely nothing. The result is obvious, time has been wasted and long hours are needed to catch up.

So why are there so many people working these long and ridiculous hours, complaining about how tired they are, and nobody cares?

'That's why I have to stay here and ensure that things are done correctly'.

I believe there are many reasons for this behaviour which you may or may not choose to acknowledge, not even to yourself. But take a break and think if any of the scenarios just may touch on the truth.

One reason for staying in the office may be due to circumstances at home. I worked in Hong Kong, in the days before 1997. many of the Chinese employees, lived in very small apartments. Their homes were often so small that it was almost impossible to have the whole family there at any one time, let alone entertain visitors. Therefore, the local Chinese seldom left work early to go home but rather lingered on, met friends in town, had dinner there and only then went home, and to bed. This did result in the grave misconception that the Chinese were very conscientious and extremely hard working. I have no intention of entertaining this discussion now, but you can see that this could be another very sound reason for staying late in the office.

Perhaps those concerned have little or no outside interests, hobbies or friends. They find themselves staying late, doing a little extra here and there. This can unknowingly develop into a habit. Suddenly, after many years they may look back and ask themselves what they had been doing over the last 10, 20 years. I have seen this often, and what is even more unfortunate is many never even reach that stage of questioning their achievements.

Some people immerse themselves in work after a major disappointment such as divorce or the death of a family member or close friend. This is probably a very good reason for doing a little extra, and many would in fact advocate this approach. I too believe this to be an effective 'protection' from grief, **"If someone is indispensable fire them"** but there are two riders to this. The temporary immersion may become a habit, and secondly why not put the extra effort in to some leisure or other activities. Remember at the outset I stated that enjoyment of life is of prime importance.

9

I believe another significant reason for this over-worked stressed-out approach is purely for effect. These individuals intentionally plan to arrive at the office before the boss and make certain that they are still there and visible when he leaves. They firmly believe that staying late working overtime makes them indispensable.

When I was an up-and-coming programmer in the early seventies, I was given a book called "The Psychology of Computer Programming", written by Gerald M. Weinberg. What remains with me today is a statement contained therein: *'If someone is indispensable, fire them'*

Before you say that's unfair, think about the statement for a moment. Have any of you in your entire working lives seen a company fold because this one 'indispensable' person has left? These indispensable individuals are frequently a manager's nightmare, proverbial pains-in-the-butt. They can absorb more management counselling and company time than the rest of the staff put together. Do you really need this? Someone once told me that the effect of an employee leaving a company is the same as the image left when you remove your hand from a bucket of water! If you have management who are impressed, or fooled by this practice, I suggest you move on!

Furthermore, if your management team that really does measure people and reward according to their visibility and the time they spend in the office, it is incumbent upon the team to assess its own attitudes and practices.

The only fair way to measure productivity accurately and fairly is by results

As an aside, staff staying late to take advantage of the office affair is not discussed in this book. You know exactly what you're doing, hopefully!

I concede there are valid reasons for working long hours, although not for extended periods. Many of those who burn the midnight oil may just be plain inefficient – useless. If this applies to you and you recognise this, you need to take some actions, because you will be found out. There is a distinct difference between those who are just out of their depth, and those who waste time during the day and need to catch up later.

The other common situation is that a company is understaffed or over committed. There are occasions where this cannot be avoided, and the short periods of extra work will be required. However, there are some managers, too many, who believe in lean and mean, and do not understand or foresee the steady degradation of performance due to overwork because of a lack of resources. I have often seen companies taking every business opportunity presented to them, and their turnover grows exponentially. But profit doesn't. Turning over £10 million per year when costs are £15 million does not add up. It's obvious yet this happens every day.

No doubt you will know the feeling having so much to do that you don't know where to start. The net result is you do nothing.

You need to maintain a healthy balance between work and play, and the *healthy* must not be underestimated. Time pressures created by technology, and the need for success (what is success anyway) play havoc with one's health. More and more people have private analysts, become stressed, have mental health issues, live on Valium, eat too much and take whatever else works for them.

My wife and I recently completed converting an old Welsh barn into two self-catering cottages. It was something neither of us had tackled before. We made use of local builders and craftsmen and were on site every day, helping, commenting or just making coffee. We made one key decision, no work after 5.30 pm and no work over weekends. Having weekends to relax, switch off and 're-charge our batteries' made the entire project more enjoyable, achievable and successful. As I have said earlier, leisure time is vitally important.

Are you one of those who burn the midnight oil without realising that your life is passing you by? You may fall into one or more of the categories mentioned above, or you may not. Be honest, if only with yourself, and then let's continue. Remember the objective of this book is to help you enjoy what you have achieved.

The Longest day is under threat.

4 - The Type of Person

"Incredibly, many people continue their old life-style, their habits even if they feel miserable, lonely, bored, inadequate or abused. Why? Of course ... because a habit is an easy place to hide"

Tom Rusk

It is not easy to define the exact profile of person most likely to display these long working characteristics. What I have done here is to group the proponents based on personal experience and observation and the experiences of others. I will no doubt incur the indignation of some but, as mentioned earlier, the intention is not to castigate, merely to demonstrate.

Common situations

There are many reasons why people work long hours, below I have identified what I believe to be the more common situations contributing to this behaviour.

Those who have lost someone close

Sometimes people who have suffered the loss of someone close through death, divorce/separation/break-up will use work to compensate. This behaviour is usually temporary but may develop into a habit.

Lonely and/or no outside interests

As the above, work is used to compensate and fill the hours between end of work and going to bed.

Not trained / qualified for the job

People who are incapable of doing the job by necessity work long hours. Generally this is easily rectified through training and or alternative more suitable work assignment.

Unhappy home life

Quite simply for these people there is no desire to go home, its sad but not uncommon. I have seen this go on for months or years on end.

Those who feel threatened because of some real or perceived disadvantage

Many who work long hours may feel at a disadvantage in some or other way, because of this they can feel that need to work longer to make a good impression and compensate. These disadvantages can be contributing factors to many of their other traits, such as not playing sport, not having hobbies, or friends.

Proverbial procrastinators, the time wasters

You know the type, some are just incapable of getting down to business until the deadline is looming and when they eventually do, it means working long hours.

Self promotion

There are those who use overtime as an opportunity to become very important in the overall scheme of things. Even before they regard themselves as indispensable, the feeling is that they are fundamental to the success of the organisation. Then the delusions of grandeur manifest themselves. They are known to use any excuse to avoid doing a proper job in the first place and then need to fix afterwards.

Everyone is equal

A relative newcomer to this group of 'longest day' workers is the mantra that believes everyone should have a chance, competition is bad and there is no such thing as being the best. This has resulted in school and university standards dropping dramatically and leads to the not trained/qualified for the job.

Pressured into working long hours

These are the people you really do want to have in your organisation. They are the ones that do their work quietly and efficiently, and on schedule. They stay late however due to the indirect pressure the above-mentioned people place on the rest of the team through their incompetence and implication of self importance.

Some common behaviours

Taking the scenario further, staff who persist in long hours develop another trait:

'It's not my fault, it's so and so's'.

They are never responsible for their own actions, the boss messed this up, all the others have gone on holiday, it wasn't clear what to do, it was incomplete and so it goes on. This dishonesty becomes a habit and develops into a personality trait. Dishonesty with oneself. This is not easy to recognise nor rectify, as it is difficult for many to look inwards and admit errors or omissions.

Many suffer the delusions of perfectionism (my opinion with which you are already familiar). The perfectionist, someone all of you have met from time to time, invariably ends up doing far more than is required without adding any value to the job or product. This is discussed in detail in the "how not to work long hours" section.

Summary

There are circumstances when hard work and long hours (NB: hard work and long hours are not synonymous) is justified. If you're saving up for a new house, a holiday or some other expensive purchase and overtime is remunerated, I'm prepared to let this go.

Unfortunately, this practice can be quite rewarding, especially when the boss or management suffer from the same syndrome or are those who readily believe in monitoring productivity on a clock. Very bad for morale. Conversely this behaviour will not work at all if the manager is one who leaves on time, plays golf, or has other outside interests. This masochistic theory on being in the office for a long time, fails unless there is someone to see it. (Like the tree that falls in the forest, if nobody is there to hear it, does it make a noise?).

A word of warning, and this warning is aimed mainly at the boss, those who work overtime frequently do a less than optimum job during normal working hours, due to tiredness, so that they can *justify* their working late and claiming the extra hours, it's a vicious circle.

All we have achieved is to perpetuate The Longest Day.

5 - How to notice this in yourself and others

"Sometimes the best way to figure out who you are is to get to that place where you don't have to be anything else"

Anon

In the previous chapter I have tried to provide a profile of the type of person that is likely to be one of those workaholics. Having accepted this, are we really able to see this behaviour in our staff or peers, or worse still, in ourselves? This last mentioned is particularly difficult because after all, we never listen, and this could not happen to me! Here I am hoping to provide you with sings of pending long hours before it actually happens.

Start by making sure that you yourself are not becoming a workaholic. Incidentally when checking yourself, you must be honest. If you think you're overweight, step on a scale, if the figures aren't good then is it the scale that is faulty?

Anyway, back to the task in hand, how do we notice the trend. We are all faced with tasks we are required to do, paying tax, applying for a passport, completing time sheets, writing thank you notes, banking, tax returns and more. Beware of the individual who perform these tasks diligently, and neatly. Any mundane task done too neatly is a possibly a sign of pending workaholism.

People who talk too much also may be exhibiting early signs of problems to come. These people talk more than listen. There is a superb line from a song by Cat Stevens called Father and Son which says;

'From the moment I could talk I was ordered to listen'.

One of the most common greetings and responses are:

'Hello, how are you?':

'Fine thanks and you?'

An indication that something is amiss is when you ask after a person's well-being and they actually tell you!

From your own point of view beware when you start to find everything you're required to do becomes a strain and a bore. When your golf handicap slips out or the kids at the local tennis club are suddenly able to thrash the pants off you, you're going in the wrong direction. If your dog barks at you when you arrive home, and you cannot motivate yourself to do anything, it's time to act.

Sit back and try to remember when you last had a good time, and if you need to think then it's too long ago, and you may be getting into the dreaded habit of too many hours in the office.

The Longest Day may be closer than you think!

PART TWO – WHAT'S THE PROBLEM?

"If you wait for perfect conditions, you will never get anything done"

Ecclesiastes

The potential reasons for the long hours syndrome have been discussed and we now know how to identify those visible attributes that make us candidates for the longest day. This was the easy part, because as with giving up smoking, the decision to quit is easy, the execution can be very traumatic. What is required is a definite decision on what we would like to do, then the implementation requires a combination of some tips and tricks and introducing some behavioural modifications that many may find difficult to accept and implement.

The ideas described below can be used by anyone in any walk of life. These ideas are not confined to the work place and I do recommend that you try to adapt your new behaviour to both your work and social life so that it becomes consistent and a part of your own personality. Regarding the work place you may find some ideas appear to be more applicable to someone in a position of authority, like a line manager, the others are more general. It is up to you to ascertain exactly how you could apply the ideas to your own situations and circumstances.

I have tried to group the various ideas into categories as some are what I would call business related fundamentals and others are more personal behaviour or attitudinal concepts. The latter appear in the Third Part of this book.

What can we do to start both achieving more and enjoying life, let's do into the details of how you can avoid The Longest Day?

---

6 - Watch those Meetings

"A meeting is an event when minutes are taken and hours are wasted"

James T Kirk

There are many challenges pertaining to meetings, and I'll attempt to deal with them all, or at least the bulk of them. Meetings are the bane of everyone's life, and yet meetings sound so very important, if you're invited to a meeting it is quite an honour!

I remember being in one of those expensive, semi-fancy hotels that are regularly frequented by the business fraternity. I was passing the reception area when a group of young business people entered the lift. One individual was very excited and as I walked past I heard him say,

"A meeting, wow, we're off to a meeting, where is it, what is it about?"

Those of you who have been around longer than most will no doubt remember the excellent business training videos produced by John Cleese. One that comes to mind was called 'Meetings Bloody Meetings' and went on to show just how disruptive and ineffective these can be.

Consider your own attendance of meetings. I would suggest that where at all possible try to avoid them. There are and will be meetings you should attend, but as a general guideline the first point of departure is don't. If you are invited then make sure you know why you were invited, what is expected of you and whether you will benefit or contribute, then attend.

If you are the one calling the meeting it may be a good idea to reaffirm in your own mind that the meeting is necessary and that only those that should be there are invited and will be present. So often we attend meetings where everyone and his dog are present, but only 10% of the attendees say anything. This may be because the subject is not pertinent to all the attendees or perhaps the meeting's objective was to gain consensus of a strategic move and the attendees are not the decision-makers.

A chairperson, as the name suggests must chair meetings. The length of the meeting can be controlled if there is an agenda and this is adhered to. Take discussions off-line, form smaller action groups or reschedule if there are subjects that require additional consideration. An old yet very effective approach is not to allow a 'General' item on the agenda. This will discourage or prohibit those who have not prepared for the meeting to have their say about something totally irrelevant or wish to use the meeting as an opportunity to moan about a long-closed item.

When to hold meetings

There is an advantage in running meetings at the correct time of day or week. What is the best time, let's first look at the various types of meetings?

- Progress review
- Planning
- Staff announcements

- Celebrations
- Debriefing (after the completion of a task or project)
- Training
- Problem solving

A further consideration is the likely mood of the meeting. Some meetings are obviously positive when there are celebrations or at the end of a very successful project. Others may not be that way, like announcements of bad results, staff retrenchments or debriefing after a failure.

One of the most difficult meetings to run are those where controversial decisions have been made affecting the entire company, for example new personnel policies are to be introduced. The best time for these meetings is last thing at the end of the week. This will prevent the inevitable groups chatting or moaning in the corridors and coffee rooms afterwards. After a meeting last thing on a Friday afternoon most people will head off home. The weekend is then used consciously or subconsciously to mull over what has been said and by the time Monday comes around you'll find most have come to terms with the news and life goes on. Should you or anyone feel strongly against the announcement, the weekend allows time for the emotion to subside and logic to prevail, so that any argument or counter proposals can be better structured. The old adage that time heals all, works.

Celebratory meetings are best held at the end of the day, so that should a party mood prevail those participants can carry on outside of normal working hours.

There are many meetings where it is essential that the attendees actively contribute and participate. Examples would be meetings called to prepare a strategy on how to grow the company, entice new clients or to resolve urgent technical problems. Such meetings require the team to be alert and creative and are best scheduled early in the morning when generally people are fresher.

Meetings that are essentially information gathering and report back, such as progress reviews can be held at any time of the day. However, this does pre-suppose that the report back information has been prepared.

Training meetings are not training courses (which are usually longer and held in formal environment, possibly off the premises), but meetings scheduled to bring people up to date on a subject or learn about a new system or product. Again we need attendees to be awake and alert, these training sessions are best held in the mornings.

Be prepared

"By failing to prepare, you are preparing to fail"

Benjamin Franklin

It is possible to reduce the time required for meetings by ensuring that all the attendees are well prepared. Ample notice of the meeting must be given, with a specific agenda and the objectives clearly stated. Where applicable make sure that those attendees required to contribute or participate actively in the meeting are well aware of exactly what is required of them. There may be those who attend for information gathering purposes only. When this happens let it be known to all concerned that persons A and B are there to listen only. This will avoid unreasonable expectations of them being raised. And please make sure that the time and place of the meeting is clearly stated, the number of people who 'get lost' looking for the meeting is frightening.

Being prepared cannot be emphasised enough. How many times can you think of where the delegates have not read the minutes, understood the topics, or have not done the prescribed homework? When this happens, the meeting is forced to spend time revisiting old topics and reminding everyone of what happened previously. The ultimate waste of time is when a group is brought together with the specific purpose of providing feedback on a document or report. The prepared team will only read and discuss contentious areas, the unprepared team will read the entire document from cover to cover, thus doing in the meeting what was clearly part of the preparation. I would suggest that should you be faced with an audience that is not prepared, reschedule for a later date, or alternatively, grant the unprepared individuals leave of absence, tell them to bugger off!

Training sessions invariably require that the delegates have a certain level of basic knowledge, without which they would be unlikely to grasp the next level of information. If you need to provide training or assistance or advice, ensure the 'student' has read the fundamentals. You can't provide half hour advice on quantum physics to someone who doesn't have the educational background.

Start the meeting on time

How many meetings have you attended when having arrived on time the start is delayed because so-and-so is running late or forgot or some other reason? I have already alluded to the fact that generally people are very tardy when it comes to time keeping. How to solve this?

Quite simple really, make it very clear in your invitation to a meeting that you will be starting strictly at the time stated and anyone late will not be admitted to the meeting, full-stop. I learnt this from a company who was recruiting members for a new business network initiative and I love it. It ruffles feathers, puts noses out of joint but boy it does work! And remember the indispensable person, should he or she be late, they will soon understand what indispensable really means.

Set a time limit

Make sure you set a time limit for the meeting and that everyone in attendance is aware of this limit. You may feel that sticking to a time limit is restrictive. It needn't be if there is a clear stated agenda and objective. What a time limit does achieve is a significant reduction in the inevitable waffle.

Another real benefit of a time limit is that all who attend can plan the rest of their day. An all-too-common excuse for long hours is that the meeting went on longer than planned and if this happens the rest of your day is affected. This is covered later in Chapter 12, Effective Use of Time.

If you plan to run a lengthy meeting of a couple of hours or more make sure that there are designated breaks. Remember people do get tired and their minds wander after a relatively short period of time (45 minutes).

You may well say that it is not always possible to know how long a certain meeting (task) will take so how can you set a time limit. This is when it is even more important to do so. Set a time limit for the meeting, after which time if there is no resolution, time for a follow-up meeting can be set aside. It is not necessary to run a meeting like a jury out on a verdict.

Everything has a time limit;

Timeless cricket test matches were played in the late 1800s until 1939. The last timeless test was between England and South Africa but had to end 'early' (after 12 days) as the England team had to catch a boat back home.

Stick to the subject (the Agenda)

We have discussed the need for an agenda and the benefit thereof. Notwithstanding this, you will find many attendees will try to use the meeting for the achievement of their own objectives. It is very easy for a meeting to start drifting, and it only takes one individual with an anecdote to set this ball rolling. The chairperson must remain alert at all times and the moment the meeting starts to wander, be strong enough to bring it back on track immediately.

Use the meeting for the purpose for which it was arranged, for example if it is a progress reporting meeting, do not use the forum to solve technical problems. If during the meeting it becomes apparent that there is a need for some research, problem solving, brainstorming, then action the necessary staff to take the task offline.

Keep proper records (minutes)

This administrative aspect of meetings is frequently overlooked or performed to the minimum level of acceptance. Worse still, many meetings are not recorded at all. I personally hate administrative work, and will, like I guess everyone else will, try to avoid it at all costs. However, I have come to understand and must admit now, that the benefit of accurate records cannot be emphasised enough.

A lawyer once told me that in cases of litigation the side with the best kept records usually wins. Legal circumstances may require one to go back months or years in a company's records to be able to prove something. It goes without saying that time wasted when no records are kept becomes significant.

Minutes of meetings are crucial to the ultimate objective of trying to work shorter hours. Minutes record decisions and actions and it is important to ensure all actions agreed upon are allocated to the correct individuals and that they in turn understand their responsibilities and deadlines. All too often actions are ignored because the details have not been written down.

The minutes taker should understand the subject matter of the meeting and be able to determine what is important and what is general chit-chat. Just asking someone without the necessary background to take minutes will not work!

An important point to remember is that you should not action anyone who is not present in the meeting. This can cause all kinds of problems; the person actioned is never informed of his or her responsibility and the task is not done. Yet down the line, the records will show that person "A" did not fulfil his or her obligation. And the poor sod wasn't even aware of this. If a person not present at the meeting is required to do something, an attendee must be made responsible for briefing that person, and the minutes should reflect this.

Proper minutes can save an awful lot time explaining and re-explaining and trying to remember what it really was that needed consideration.

A final point, 'not cricket' as the British would say but nevertheless real. The person who writes the minutes is in control. If there is anything in the minutes (which must always be distributed to the attendees and others) that is incorrect or misleading, it is incumbent upon the reader to raise the objection. As so many are too lazy to do so, or forget when the next meeting comes around, the content of the minutes stand, and cannot be refuted later.

Select the attendees carefully

Whenever you call a meeting make sure you know something about each of the attendees and why they should be present. Within your own department or group meeting this is a simple matter. When there is a need to extend invitations to others, you need to be more careful. Other than making sure the attendees are prepared, the right level, and in addition to the other points discussed above, you need to beware of potential hidden agendas that may prevail. This sounds political, and it is. Some people may be there to grandstand, others because they think they have been empowered to participate, (which might mean your meeting is run according to unionist ideals). But why not use this knowledge to your own advantage; there is nothing in the rulebook that prohibits you from planting your own allies.

But don't get too embroiled in the politics at the expense of what we're trying to achieve here. When the meeting is held with the right people, plus all the other points discussed above, you'll be surprised how quickly you'll be able to complete the agenda.

A fellow business consultant gave me an interesting insight to meetings. He said that if you observe carefully you will notice that meeting can run awry when the subject matter of a topic drops to a lower intellectual level. Discussions will take much longer as more of the attendees will be able to contribute.

Here is an example thereof.

"The tendency of democracies is, in all things, to mediocrity"

James Fenimore Cooper

Some time ago I was advising an organisation who were running a building restoration project. Their meetings were well planned, held regularly and agendas were circulated. When the subject for discussion was related to project finance, only a few of the attendees contributed. The subject was dealt with quickly and the meeting moved on. Another agenda item related to building design and planning. Here more people commented as many had been involved in the initial design ideas. This subject took a little longer. When it came to choosing the colour of table cloths in the dining room everyone leapt in with their own opinions. That took 45 minutes to discuss I am not exaggerating; the point is a meeting addressing specialist subjects should be attended by the specialists. Anyone else who needs to know what is being discussed can read the minutes. Over the nearly 2 years I was there I believe we could have saved hundreds of hours.

Summary

Someone once told me that any simple problem can be made insoluble if enough meetings are held to discuss it. There's certainly truth in this statement.

However, meetings are inevitable. They can extremely valuable but in my experience are frequently a waste of time. The best advice I can give you is to avoid them whenever possible. But as you know this is not easy because of what was said earlier. The major time wasters are related to time schedules, agendas, (or lack thereof) and having the right attendees. Finally the chairperson must be able to control the meeting, this presupposes that the chairperson is of sufficient seniority within in the organisation.

Manage these and you will avoid The Longest Day in the extreme!

7 - Do not overlook Planning

"Plan your dive and dive your plan"
A well-known scuba diving saying

I believe planning is a lost art, or possibly not understood in the first place. Many people treat planning as a waste of time. They receive instructions to do something and start right away, without any thought of how they are going to do the job and the best approach to be followed.

I have yet to discover a situation where even a minimal amount of planning or thought is not required.

Plan before you start

When one arrives at home after purchasing a new smart phone, or washing machine or motor car, what is the first thing we do? Plug it in, switch it on; and then see what happens. Most of us do not first sit down and read the instruction booklet. (From this comes the well-worn cliché, 'When all else fails read the manual'). You may ultimately succeed in setting up your new appliance, but rest assured it will take you a lot longer than if you had spent time reading the manual, in other words planning.

In the computer industry, in the old days before PCs, computers were big, expensive and slow, and the need for careful planning was forced by complexity on the one hand and the fact that opportunities for testing were limited. I have noticed that the current breed of software developers appears to ignore the planning phase completely. The recent spate of large computer system failures in some of the banks and other institutions come to mind.

You will probably have noticed that those who begin a task at a great rate invariably complete their assignments long before anyone else. These individuals are then praised for their speed and commitment to duty. But a task is not complete until the product or service has been tested or delivered. Invariably there will be errors, or features that have been overlooked and to correct these will take an inordinate amount of time. Why, let me give a very simple example. If you have been asked to make a steak and kidney pie, and you forget the kidneys, you must make another pie. The ultimate completion date slips severely.

If you know exactly what is required (see Do Only What is Required later) you will know what you need and how you are going to achieve this. The overall time required to complete the task will be considerably reduced.

Furthermore, proper planning will identify any potential problems and aspects which may have been overlooked during the specification or design phase. Errors will always occur, but the earlier an error is encountered the easier it will be to rectify. The 'bull at a gate' approach simply cannot pre-empt problems.

We frequently ask ourselves why we never have time to do things right the first time, and yet we always have time to fix it later? The reason is simple, we don't plan.

Understand what is required

How is it possible to start a job unless you know and understand exactly what the end product should be? Sounds stupid yet this happens in most cases. By exactly I mean what it looks like, what it is going to do, how it's going to work, who will be using it and a lot more.

The person for whom the product is intended is the customer and his or her requirements must be written down and accepted by the customer, by way of a signature. These requirements must be specific.

Some years ago the French train operator SNCF has discovered that 2,000 new trains it ordered at a cost of 15bn Euros ($20.5bn; £12.1bn) are too wide for many regional platforms. This embarrassing blunder cost the rail operator over 50m Euros ($68.4m; £40.6m). The reason, not all the requirements were considered.

When you know exactly what you are going to do, you can estimate the time and the associated cost of the job accurately. After the customer has accepted the final description (the Requirements Document) any changes to the If you don't have all the information you can make a mess of it and it may cost considerably more.

Risk Analysis

During the planning process you should always look at the potential risks which may affect the ability to deliver the completed project on time. there are many to consider, the supply of materials, the weather, the availability of staff, the lead time required for certain legal requirements such as planning, environmental impact studies and more. Then there are the health and safety considerations regarding personal safety.

Understanding what the risks are allows you to schedule and cost more accurately and mitigate the risks where possible. It may turn out that the project cannot go ahead, and the best time to find this out is before commencing.

Plan for contingencies

Murphy's law prevails, and things will go wrong no matter how well you prepare, plan, check and double check. When you plan, allow for things to go wrong.

Take this example, you're going to a job interview for a position you really want. The interview is set for 10 am, not far away. You know the drive takes 20 minutes, so you leave a 9-40 am. But lo and behold there is an accident on your route, and your forced detour means you arrive late. It's not your fault, or is it? In that case you may well get away with it, but how about another scenario. You are required to appear in a court of law, being late could have serious consequences. If your company was responding to a tender, tender submission times are set in stone, a delay due to traffic will not suffice.

"Leave is a right, when you take it is a privilege"

Anon

I have seen many project plans, which at first glance appear to be comprehensive and well thought out. Closer scrutiny however shows that every single minute of every day of every week is allocated. This is where so many of the best-laid plans go astray. People get sick, they take leave (and in many countries this is mandatory and unused leave cannot be carried forward), they have unscheduled personal chores like visiting the dentist or having the car serviced, and so it goes on. Then there are statutory public holidays. Finally, no one is fully productive 100% of the time, we all suffer good and bad days. In the final analysis when all the above is considered, the average working year only has between 180 and 200 days. If this is not considered when planning then deadlines will not be met, and the additional effort required to rectify the resultant situation will be far higher than the original effort required.

You will remember my earlier comments, if delivery is promised for a certain time, and this deadline is met, extreme satisfaction from all parties is guaranteed.

Plan free time

I am not talking about planning what you intend to do when you get home or after work. I'm talking about planning to have time during the day for yourself, and this time is not for running private errands.

Set aside a certain amount of time per day or week, wherein you plan, read all your emails, catch up on correspondence, do administrative work, and finally, and most importantly, think. (If you make use of a network scheduling system whereby others in the organisation can book your free time, then this private time of yours must reflect as not available to others).

Everyone needs this thinking time, regardless of position. In a managerial or supervisory position, you probably need more time, thinking not only about your job but those of your staff; who is best for which task, how to counsel or discipline a person, and the many other management functions. I have noticed that many job advertisements for management positions state that the applicants must have appropriate technical skills.

"The way to get things done

is not to mind who gets

the credit for doing them"

Benjamin Jowett

Clearly there are too many out there who do not understand that management is a thinking planning game, with the responsibility of ensuring delivery and success.

Ronald Reagan was regarded by many as an inadequate president, yet I believe he truly understood the meaning of management. He was quoted as saying;

"You should surround yourself with experts, listen to them all, and then take the final decision."

You as a manager need to plan this time. As a non-manager this thinking, free time is equally important, so plan for it.

Summary

In summing up, planning is key to reducing hours. I do not believe that it is possible to immediately embark on a project without knowing exactly how you are going to proceed. Lack of planning will definitely exacerbate The Longest Day.

8 - Common Business Sense

"It is a pity that common sense is so uncommon"

Anon

The ideas discussed in this section I have called "Common Business Sense" items. They may not be hard and fast business rules but should be regarded as traditional business practices. Common sense requires a little thought, and a little patience.

'Stick to the knitting'

Translated this means you and your staff should follow the business objectives of the company. Stick with what you know and are good at. This concept is not new but is frequently overlooked or ignored completely.

It is all too easy to get side tracked especially when a problem occurs with a task or function that has been delegated to a third party. The natural reaction is to want to do it yourself. (Remember the 'If you want it done right you must do it yourself' person). This is dangerous and often invokes an emotional reaction which can lead to significant implications being overlooked. In addition, the cost of gearing up for a new product or service, especially if it is unfamiliar to your company, can be very expensive.

The key is making sure you have the right people for the right job within the focus and mission statement of the company.

As was said earlier much of what is contained here is applicable to one's non-business activities as well. A simple example, your house needs painting. You have neither the inclination nor the skills, so you retain the services of a painter. Again, it's merely recoganising what one is good at and then obtaining assistance in the areas where your own skills are inadequate.

There will always be times where you need to resolve a problem yourself, for many reasons like money or when you are nowhere near anyone who can provide the expert assistance required. Or you may want to tackle something new purely out of interest. This interest is part of the natural human desire to experiment and try new things, and without this attitude we would not be anywhere near as advanced technologically as we are now. It is because of this human trait that businesses do expand and branch into new markets.

This may sound contradictory, but it is merely identifying reality. Generally speaking in a company, it is important to remember what the business is, and stick to it. Many successful companies outsource activities that do not form part of their core business.

Delegate or suffocate

The ability to delegate, to let go, appears to be a major problem for so many people. I wonder if this is merely a syndrome of being scared to delegate because:

- the person will do this better than you

- you don't understand the job and therefore cannot explain it (bear this one in mind)
- it shows a weakness and you think your boss will think you are inadequate
- it's a great job and you want to do it.

Delegation does not mean dumping a task on someone else and then walking away. Delegation is morale boosting, it provides opportunities for individuals to attain new skills, it builds trust, and spreads the workload.

"If you really want to grow as an entrepreneur, you've got to learn to delegate"
Richard Branson.

The first thing to remember is that you cannot delegate responsibility, and therefore the ultimate success or failure of the task remains with you. It is essential that you explain exactly what is required of the person to whom you are delegating. Spend as much time as you can during this phase as it is upon this that success or failure rests. It also shows that you still have an interest in the task even though you're giving it to someone else.

What we frequently overlook is the motivation factor of allowing someone else to tackle an important job. It is based on trust, and you can only delegate effectively if you trust the person to whom you are handling the task. Delegation must be to an appropriate person who has the necessary skills for the tasks, the ability to understand the role and then to report back to you accurately and timeously.

Another beware point, do not delegate and then spend the rest of the time looking over the persons shoulder. This wastes everyone's time and will certainly annoy the person doing the job.

At the beginning of this section I suggested that many can't delegate because they do not have the necessary knowledge of the job in hand. Managers do not need to have in-depth detailed knowledge of the job, they need to understand the overall concept, the required deliverable and most importantly they need to know what they don't know, and then delegate accordingly.

A final point on delegation. Many managers believe that having highly competent successful people on their team will put their own jobs in jeopardy. In truth the better your subordinates perform, the higher up the corporate ladder they push you.

Earlier we discussed the need for private time to think and plan. One of the easiest ways to achieve this is by effective delegation. Let us remember the objective of all this, to have more free time to play.

Use the right people for the job

Such an obvious statement and yet so frequently do we make the mistake of using the wrong people for the wrong tasks. Much of this stems from laziness; he is available so let's use him. Another foible is that we omit to train or inform people and yet happily delegate tasks for which they are neither prepared nor educated.

Another mistake we frequently make, because of our reluctance to delegate, is to use over qualified people for tasks. We justify this by suggesting that if you use a heavyweight you will get a good job done. This is not always true, as to the heavyweight the task is boring, and the heavyweight may come with a heavyweight salary.

Taking availability a little further, be sure that anyone to whom you assign a particular task or project will be available for the duration of the task and is not due to fly off to Siberia or somewhere for a prolonged vacation. Nothing annoys a customer more than having a host of different people to deal with on their specific project or situation.

When making use of consultants, make sure you control them and make sure they know exactly what is expected of them. Otherwise there can be resentment by your own staff, especially as the inclination is to listen to outsiders because they are just that. Many companies are heard to ignore the advice of their own staff, hire outsiders at exorbitant fees, who ultimately tell them the same things. There is a lot of truth in the statement,

'You hire a consultant to use your watch to tell you the time.'

From a purely commercial point of view it doesn't make sense to use highly paid staff to do mundane things. Use the right people for the job and consider delaying a task until the right one is available rather than tinkering around with the wrong person. We want the job done once correctly, so that our free time remains free.

Schedule properly

I make a distinction between planning and scheduling. Planning is the process of thinking and working out how to go about a task or set of tasks, scheduling is identifying the time and resources required to complete these tasks together in a written schedule with completion dates.

Scheduling is a very important task and requires a certain amount of experience and skill. If possible, and this depends on your level or position within the organisation, do your own schedules. Now I do realise that life isn't always that simple, and many deadlines are imposed on us by other people or circumstances. What the issue is here, a deadline set and accepted by the person who will do the job is far more likely to be met, than one imposed from above with no regard for whether it is feasible or not. Remember that if the deadline is regarded as impossible at the outset, there is absolutely no incentive to even try to meet it, why kill oneself for nothing.

A common scheduling practice is to work backwards from a pre-determined completion date. This 'reverse squeeze' pleases the recipients of the deliverable but is seldom successful. (There was one project where the backward squeeze was successful, as the end date was caste in solid rock; Y2K, the preparation for the Year 2000).

Note: Many people believe that since there were no disasters, no planes falling out of the sky etc. Y2K was a hoax. In fact Y2K was very real, there were thousands of people (computer programmers) working day and night for a number of years to ensure that there were no disasters.

Planning and scheduling often creates conflicts in certain jobs, so beware. A common management statement is;

'I cannot time manage as I am always available for my staff, my door is always open'.

This sounds fine until you find the real management functions such as administration and personnel tasks fall behind. A suggestion is to schedule certain times of the day for your own tasks, and other times when your door is open. If during this period the open door is not used, you have the extra time to catch up. Another trick is to schedule dead periods in your own diary, as mentioned earlier.

Keep everyone informed

Tell people what's happening. If the company is facing stiff market competition from a new market entrant, tell the staff. You need not to divulge all the nitty-gritty details but sharing the overall situation with them allows them to better understand some of the very difficult decisions you may be forced to make. This is fundamental to everything we're discussing here. Remember that the objective is to cut down unnecessary time spent at work, and therefore anything that saves time and effort is worthwhile. The same applies to your friends and families.

What do you do when you hit a snag and you know you will be unable to deliver the product by the scheduled date or you will not be able to make that important appointment at the end of the month? If you take the soft (scared) route and keep quiet until the customer or friends calls to find out why the product didn't arrive or where you were at the end of the month, its too late, you have damaged your credibility and reputation. Call the person concerned soon as you know you've a problem and tell them that you cannot do whatever you promised, the reason and what you will do to minimise the damage. This is particularly important when the fault is your own making.

Answer email and telephone calls. I don't believe there is anything more annoying than leaving messages and not having them answered. If you have promised to call someone that afternoon to give them a progress report, and there is nothing to report, phone them, and tell whoever that there is no news. Do not leave them wondering what has happened. The applies to all means of communication, if you said you would call, write, email, text then do it!

It is time for a dig at another industry. I'm sure all of you have favourite punching bags; in my circle of friends, Personnel Agencies come under fire. And the common complaint is that you, as a prospective client, never know where you stand regarding your application. When challenged the inevitable agency response is that there are so many applications, we do not have time to respond, especially to those who will not be successful. A very simple solution to this would be to use standard email responses. One such consultancy replies immediately with a standard response that says,

'We will not respond if your application is not successful, and if you don't hear from us for 2 weeks, expect the worst'.

This is better than nothing?

Be honest and forthright, you'll be surprised how many potential confrontational or sensitive issues can be disarmed by saying;

'I'm sorry its late, but I will be able to do this by then'.

In the context of work, be truthful with yourself and then with your peers and seniors. Reporting based on what you feel they would like to hear is extremely dangerous and will have serious repercussions. Then the overtime starts, and this is exactly what we're trying to avoid.

Manage peoples' expectations

Our lives are based on performing activities and looking forward to events. These events incorporate all sorts of occasions, holidays, birthdays, visits from far-off relatives, getting married, collecting a new car and so the list goes on. In all cases we can wait for the events because we are under the impression that they will happen at predetermined times. In many cases these times (deadlines) are given to us by those controlling the activities leading up to these events.

When you place an order for a book, you are given a delivery date. This date may or may not be to your liking but having accepted the deal, your expectation is set; the book will arrive in 2 months' time. A long time to wait, but nevertheless that's what you do. If or when this deadline is missed one's

Communication is the key to managing people's expectations

disappointment and anger is significant. And all this could have been avoided if the first delivery date was guaranteed and had a bit of float in case of hiccups. (Remember the Planning for Contingencies above).

The key is to manage your customers' expectations. It will save a lot of heartbreak, explanations and time. Remember stress wastes time.

Do only what is required

I can immediately hear many of you screaming about going the 'extra mile', customer service, a little extra and so on. Nothing that I propose here contradicts this magnanimous attitude, so cool down and read on. We all want our customers to be happy, and yes, you can go the extra mile, just make sure that the proverbial mile is not a cross-country trip, or even worse the start of a never–ending problem.

Most important here is to listen to the brief and understand exactly what is required and the rationale behind the request. It is at this stage you are welcome to question the reasoning, suggest alternatives and provide the professional advice expected of you. But once this has been done, the specified task must be completed as agreed.

Here are examples of what may happen if you ignore this advice:

You are a landscape gardener and have been retained to develop an indigenous garden at the bottom of a property. The specifications and measurements are provided and you start the job. Half way through you feel that the measurements were a little restrictive and you notice that if you extend the garden by 20 feet the added effect would be brilliant. You make the change, and the property owner is furious. Why, because the extra area you prepared was allocated for the construction of a swimming pool. The net result is that you have not met the requirement, have probably taken longer than expected, and the new garden will inevitably go over budget.

Now for the perfectionist. In my opinion the common perfectionist is one who seldom if ever understands the meaning of perfection. Some years ago I employed an administrative assistant. New on the job this young

"The pursuit of perfection often impedes improvement"

George Will

lady stated categorically that she was a perfectionist, everything had to be perfect. Hold that thought for a moment. Her first task was to sort out the company's filing system. Bear in mind this was a small company, and the filing system was paper-based, manual and in held alphabetical order. We asked her to make sure that labels on the files matched the contents therein. Should this not be the case the contents and /or the labels had to be corrected. If there was a need for additional files, she should create them. The reorganisation of this simple system took the new assistant more than a week; it should have taken a couple of days. Why, because every file label had been re-written in ink, in the style of old English script, taking hours. The information in many of the files had not changed and there few other corrections to be made. Legible handwritten labels would have sufficed. To us all we needed was to be able to identify the contents of a file from the label. To her however what she had done was perfection.

Perfection is not prettier than necessary. If someone phones your office while you're out and leaves a message, which says:

'Fred phoned, please phone back, the number is....'

This message, taken by a perfectionist would be typed; by a normal person this would be handwritten. If the objective of the message is to convey such, then how is a typed message better than a hand written one? This is not to say that aesthetics is a waste of effort, not at all, but in the right place. Remember, do what is required.

The other risk with perfectionists is that they find it difficult to take criticism, constructive or otherwise, and become very defensive and closed to suggestions. Frequently the perfectionist is protective or his/her work and spends far too much time over embellishing something that should be straight forward. Quite simply, if a task is clearly understood and delivered accordingly, is this not real perfection?

You will find later in the book that if you achieve the objective set for any task, no more can be asked. The risks of not doing what is requested results in time wasting, additional costs, more resources and an unhappy customer. And the final insult may be that the customer doesn't even notice the extra effort!

A point to ponder, if you do go overboard striving for the extra mile you may find yourself making the customer's problem your own. Don't.

Take decisions and then make them work

"The best argument against democracy is a 5-minute discussion with the average voter"
Winston Churchill

There are seldom situations which can be resolved by one approach only, most have several different alternatives. If you subscribe to management by committee, then 50% will want something done one way, and the other 50% another way. What you need is a decision to be made and once this is done, make the decision work.

When there are multiple ways of doing something, the alternatives must be considered, quickly. You want to avoid lengthy discussions after which those not in favour of the ultimately selected choice may intentionally or inadvertently disrupt the project. (sounds like Brexit!) Short discussions don't allow time to think and develop a position, and as we all know most of us react well to decisiveness. Make the decision and once this is done cease all further discussions on the merits of the decision.

Learn to Prioritise properly

Priorities, what to do now, what to do next, who to call first, are some of the many decision one is faced with every day. The ability to establish what is important, what is not important and then to prioritise accordingly is a tremendous skill to have. This is not easy, especially when there is a lot to do. Initially many may believe everything is important (this sounds good to the boss) but this not true. This is where the ability to prioritise comes in.

Every project has any number of sub-tasks which together make up the project deliverable. Some are dependent on previous sub-tasks being completed. Others have no dependencies and can be tackled any time within the overall project schedule. Those that are dependent upon others are the important task and require more attention. These are the fundamental building blocks upon which the project deliverable is based.

Now for a tricky one, a project is running late, and you cannot deliver the promised product or service on time. What do you do, delay another project so that you can redirect resources, do you leave out parts of the project or at least delay them until later?

A little risk analysis won't go amiss here. If you are faced with identifying which customer to service first and which you need to ask to wait, you may take this decision based on value of the business, size and length of time you've had the client and the visibility of the client. (Please make sure that you look after existing customers before potential prospects).

Then if you must deliver an incomplete solution, here are some areas you can address when faced with an impossible and immovable deadline:

•   Aesthetics. These pretty add-ons are frequently time consuming and do little to enhance the function of the deliverable.

•   Nice-to-haves. These are non-essential aspects covering functions that would easily be able to be done with existing processes and procedures.

•   Anything that is only likely to be used in exceptional circumstances.

Please note that for any part of the deliverable you delay or omit, there is an alternative (maybe manual) way of performing the function.

When faced with delaying or omitting tasks, you must not to compromise on the other tasks and end up doing everything to a 70% level. Tasks must be dropped or delayed in their entirety so that what is still delivered works 100% correctly in its own right.

Finally, just because you have saved the day by some smart footwork, the task still must be completed at some stage or other.

Summary

This was a lot to think about and some points may be a little difficult to employ. Initially focussing on communication, managing people's expectations and making decisions you'll find you will make huge strides into eliminating The Longest day

9- Effective use of modern (and old-fashioned) tools

"A computer will not make a good manager out of a bad manager. It makes a good manager better faster and a bad manager worse faster"

Edward Esber

In years gone by the fastest means of communication was mail (postman delivering letters, not email). There was the Pony Express, and mail ships driven by sail, letters could take months to reach their destinations. The phone came next and this speeded up local and international communications. Following this we had telex, then fax and finally email. Now we are being faced with such incredible communications capabilities and apps that there is no excuse for not telling someone something. This and with the accompanying technology life can be fun!!??

Be careful. There are two ways to approach technology, one is for the sake of it, and the other is driven by the need to do something more efficiently. The latter is probably the better reason for pursuing technology, but again, beware, some of these labour savers are anything but that. With all the apps available today some people are using apps to manage apps!

Be that as it may, generally speaking the tools we have at our disposal today, when used effectively, are excellent time and effort savers, with the added benefit of accuracy. Use them.

Internet

The internet, one of the most influential technologies of today, and it cannot be ignored. The internet provides a cost-effective means of communication for everyone.

There are so many applications that it is impossible to discuss them all here. We are trying to save time, and one of the tremendous benefits is the continuous availability of information, better and faster than any library. Research has never been easier. Add this to the other benefits of shopping, making reservations for whatever, banking and communicating, the use of Internet is essential to our cause.

PCs and tablets

Quite honestly the use of PCs should not require discussion. If you are less than seventy-five years old, literate, and you still cannot find your way around a PC and the common applications now, you are not part of this world. However, it is worthwhile to revisit some aspects of the PC.

Microsoft and others have developed some amazing Apps (applications) which are able to do 'anything'. In the business environment the ability to prepare business proposals and presentations is easy and the results can be extremely professional. (Some of us do still remember type-writers). And these Apps are being used and understood by more and more people. Where is this leading?

Because these tools are so easy to use, and fun to use, the tendency is to spend too much time either learning about all the options the app provides or creating something that far exceeds the required result. (see the section on perfectionism).

I would subscribe that the most effective use of PCs is to know what can be done, and as soon as there is a task that can be best performed by an app, learn and use it accordingly.

Email, friend or villain?

Personally I like email but it is possibly one of the worst handled technology tools of today (and here I include mobile phones). It is not unheard of to receive literally hundreds of emails a day. Very few of us have the time, or inclination to read them and the benefits of this technology are totally negated by the abuse thereof.

I met a senior person in an international organisation who never read his email. He never had the time. His secretary read his mail, and then gave him a daily summary of the important issues (as she interpreted the messages). Is that the way we want to operate? It saved time for him, but the damage to relationships and overlooked problems and opportunities cannot be measured.

When there are mails to and fro on a subject, the common practice is it continue to 'reply' thus retaining the history for background purposes. The idea is sound but can be taken to extremes. On the other hand, there is nothing more infuriating than when someone answers an email without replying to the original.

The ability to copy many recipients on a subject is frequently abused. The reasons given for this behaviour is "to make sure that everyone who needs to know is kept informed". The reality is many cases is that:

- the sender wants to cover his or her backside
- sender is *sucking up* to the senior management
- get someone else into trouble (a message asking an individual why a particular task was not done, and then copying the message to management.)
- curry favour in disputes

Be selective and try to put the subject matter clearly in the heading. And only use 'Urgent' when it is such. We want to save time remember?

Finally, PLEASE answer emails, even if it is only an acknowledgement of receipt thereof. If the email contains more than one question please answer *all* the questions, not just the first one. If I send an email I would like to know it has been received and that the contents thereof were acceptable. Many do not respond or even acknowledge and it drives me insane.

If you phone someone and ask them a question, and they provide the answer, do you just put the phone down?

Voice Mail

Don't you just love voice mail, you phone to speak to someone at their work place and you're put through to his or her voice mail.

"Hello, you have reached the voice mail of...I'm unable to take your call, leave a message after the beep".

That's it, no *"hold on or dial zero if you want to speak to an operator"*.

At this stage you do not know if the person concerned is in the office, and busy, down the passage, out for the day, away on leave, available at that number, or dead!

I wonder if you realise some voice mail systems, maybe all of them, have no way of prioritising messages. Messages are stored in incoming sequence, and can only be retrieved in reverse, oldest to newest sequence. That's fine except that there is no quick way of retrieving urgent messages without listening to the entire recording.

Video-conferencing

This was initially an underused form of communication, probably because at the outset, Video Conferencing was considered expensive. Nowadays we have Skype, webinars, YouTube and other video conferencing tools are available to all.

In the global village where any business can cross many international boundaries, video conferencing is infinitely more cost and time effective than flying groups of people half way across the world.

Mobile/Cell (Smart) Phones

I doubt if there has been an invention that has captured the world market more quickly than the cellular (mobile) phone. Have you ever wondered how we ever operated without them? After all people now need to take very important calls in the theatre, Grand Slam tennis tournaments, and at a night at the opera!

"Cell phone users irritate more than Herpes"

Anon

Sarcasm and bad manners aside, cell phones are here to stay. Although very much part of today, there are still those die-hards who refuse point-blank to either use cell phones or phone someone on their mobile phones. The excuse here is that you do not know where they are, and they might be busy? More and more households have mobile communication only, no land line. Why not make use of a simple time saving tool if it is available?

There is a distinct advantage in being able to contact someone sooner rather than later. These phones do work and have their place on the market, use them to your advantage.

Smart phones are superb; I like the access to email when I'm away, the diary, the search facilities, contactless payments and more.

But (and I heard a line in a movie that "everything before the **but** is bullshit"!), one's entire life is held on a small piece of plastic and metal, easy to break, easy to steal, easy to hack and then from there it's all downhill. We are talking about saving time and not working too long, lose your phone and then the time wasting begins.

And here's another but; one must control the phone, not the other way around as is the common practice. Have you noticed the moment a person picks up a phone they become stupid, if they are walking they veer all over the place, if they are talking they cannot stay still and look as though they need a loo? They become impervious to all around them. Some take it further and speak very loudly as if believing those around want to listen to their conversations?

Social Media

This is the bane of my life and I am very pleased that I did not have to grow up in the modern society. That said, social media is here to stay (for now?) and we must accept that. What we must not let happen is that social media controls our lives to the detriment of our working lives. A tweet, text, video does not require an immediate response. Just like the telephone, you do not have to answer it.

"Social media sites create an illusion of connectivity"

Malay Shah

Apps

I want to dedicate a section to apps because they are an enigma. There are so many, (thousands everyday) by companies and individuals to solve all sorts of problems.

Most apps today are solutions looking for a problem

I attended a presentation delivered by a self-proclaimed app expert regarding the use of apps and the benefits she gained from using them. I lost count of how many she used every day. She had apps telling her what do buy for dinner, apps that told friends and family when she was half-way home, three quarters of the way home and at home. She had apps for to-do lists, apps for navigation, apps that 'made coffee 5 minutes after she arrived at the office'. By her own admission she spent hours a day managing these apps and did have apps that coordinated (managed) other apps. I give up.

There are some excellent ones, use them wisely. They are there to save time and effort, not double it.

Summary

We have discussed several of the tools that are available to you, and there are many more that may suit your own specific circumstances. Technology plays a big part in becoming more efficient. Use it and any tools wisely and they will keep The Longest Day at bay.

PART THREE – CHANGES YOU CAN MAKE

Your behaviour is a choice; it isn't who you are

Vanessa Diffenbaugh

In this chapter I introduce ideas whereby you can make a difference simply by acting differently to everyday situations. Some are behavioural changes, others relate to the organisation of your social and work life. Some ideas are easy to implement, others not so. For you to succeed you need to be honest with yourself and others and not afraid of being assertive if necessary. You may well face opposition but hang in there. One of the biggest causes of conflict is that the recipient has not fully grasped the message. A very effective way of overcoming these obstacles is to explain the rationale behind your actions, and the intended outcome.

---

10 - Change your pattern of behaviour

"Only the wisest and the stupidest of men never change"

Confucius

Anything we want to achieve will require certain changes in the way we think and talk and interact with our family, friends and colleagues. Many of these changes will be subtle and may not even be noticed by others. Other changes required may be extremely difficult for you to implement and can result in abuse and disbelief from those who know you well. Incidentally it is always easier to make a personal change, physical such as a major hairstyle alternation, or a behavioural change, when you have moved location or joined another company. Your new colleagues and friends upon meeting you will not know that this is the 'new' you.

An essential part of reducing the long hours syndrome, is the ability to say "NO". If you have always been the one to accept anything, you will have to learn to say no. Too often I have seen people snowed under due to their inability to say no. This will not be easy but is a must.

Ask for Help

This is so simple and yet very few are prepared to do this. The reasons are normally that one is scared to admit an inability to do something, scared that the boss may see this as a sign of weakness, worried that the response will be, *just work harder'*.

(At this point take a short thinking break, the 'work harder' statement belies many other inefficiencies covered throughout this book, and you may have to re-look at your own participation in a company that encourages or condones stupid statements like work harder).

Asking for help will alert the powers that be that there is a potential problem which may need attention. It displays a certain maturity when someone can ask for help, this is not a sign of weakness.

When we are falling behind, we inevitably think of adding resources. In reality this seldom helps. A common and very effective solution in most cases is to review and reschedule in line with priorities.

Do not forget that most people are flattered when asked for help - this can be very motivational.

Think ahead

I know that I have advocated that you should do what is required and no more. This must not be taken too simplistically. It is incumbent upon one to do the job, to provide some insight to the overall objectives and make sure you know where your task fits in the greater picture. If you notice something that you know will need attention in the future, raise it immediately. It is always easier to rectify a problem earlier rather than later. Prevention is certainly better than cure, and again the time spent here will be far less than will be required to fix the situation later.

Nothing has angered me more than discovering a worker doing something which is so obviously incorrect, like for example laying a new carpet right on top of a under-floor power outlet. When questioned as why this was done the smart-arse replies, 'but the plans didn't mention this'.

Thinking ahead is really part of the planning cycle which we have already discussed and can make an enormous difference to the time and effort required. I would suggest that you try to make this 'thinking' process a way of life.

Do not worry

Worrying causes stress and stress is unhealthy and one cannot function logically if under stress. Prolonged or very high stress can cause panic, and this deteriorates into a situation completely out of control. There are far too many people in the world suffering from stress-related illnesses.

This is easier said than done, and certainly many people are inherent worriers. The key is not to worry about anything that you either cannot or do not intend to do anything about it.

For example, you wake up one morning and find that your car will not start. This in itself is not a major problem except that you plan to go away for the weekend, by car, and it is Wednesday already. You get a lift to work, phone around and book the car for a service for the following day. You have now done all that you can, and therefore there is no need to worry any more about it. Or you could decide to work on the car yourself that evening when you get home. Again, having made a decision, there is no need to worry, (at least until the evening).

Should there be a real problem as there always will be, try not to pass this pressure on to all around you. Pressure and stress are contagious, undue pressure causes people to panic, cut corners and make errors. And these errors are less likely to be discovered, as one's memory under stress is confused to say the least.

"Worry often gives a small thing a big shadow"
Swedish Proverb

The same approach must be taken for projects, for it is here that so many hard-working martyrs shine. The project slips due to unforeseen circumstances, (no planning for contingencies) and the pressure rises. To make up for lost time the project staff are tempted into taking short cuts. Overtime sets in, everyone works their butts off, and finally the product is delivered, late, but with the same charge to the customer. Your company of course ran at a loss. And here comes the *coup de graz*. All the people on the project are rewarded for the extra effort they put in. They screwed up, they had to fix the problems, they cost the company plenty, and then they were rewarded for all their extra effort!!! Please don't laugh but I was once asked to reward people who had screwed up and then worked late to fix the stuff-up. Needless to say, I refused.

It is not possible to avoid all worry unless you're a total automaton but try to reduce it wherever possible. Worry, stress and panic are a complete waste of time and effort. You can reduce the risks of stress by planning, thinking ahead and then taking decisions, all of which have already been discussed above.

Don't make promises you can't keep

Not only is this possibly the most irritating thing anyone has to put up with, it invariably requires additional time and effort to keep making excuses as to why this job has not been done.

Do not under any circumstances make promises on behalf of others. Many such promises are made with the best will in the world and the damage control required afterwards will be significant.

"The only person to get everything done by Friday was Robinson Crusoe."

Anon

Let me cite an example, you are a salesman for a company, and are meeting with one of your customers. During the discussion, it transpires that the customer has been waiting for a one of your technical staff to provide an answer to a specific problem. The salesman, always there to please says" *"Don't worry, I'll speak to Bill, (the technician) and get him to phone you by the end of today"*.

So far so good, and the customer relaxes and feels happy. What could go wrong?

I'll tell you, a) Bill is ill, b) Bill is away, c) the telephone service is disrupted, and a host of other possibilities. The result is that Bill does not phone, and then who takes the flak from the customer. A far better approach is offering to speak to Bill if you can, failing which you'll leave a note. Then suggest that the customer follows up himself or alternatively provide another name for the customer to contact.

We could discuss this ad infinitum, the message is simple, do not make promises you can't keep, and if for reasons completely beyond your control, like a nuclear war, and an earthquake, then call the person to whom you promised, and explain immediately.

Honest communication, telling like it is and will be, must prevail. And remember, do not promise something that is dependent on something beyond your control.

Summary

In a nutshell if you do not over commit yourself, you are not making promises you can't keep. This will reduce the need to worry and allow you to take control over The Longest Day.

11 - Effective use of time

"One thing you can't recycle is wasted time."

Anon

I do not intend to discuss the formal aspects of time management here. Time management has been around for a long time, there are courses aplenty on the subject. There are Time Management diaries and other related tools readily available.

Effective use of time I am talking about here is how you arrange your day, and how you can, just by being 'selfish', reduce time wasting and use the additional hours gained for leisure activities.

Don't change appointments

I get the impression that today's person cares little for sticking to appointments and thinks nothing of cancelling and delaying for whatever reason. I also think mobile phones contribute to this trend as it is so easy to phone and say I'm running late. Those who do this then feel good, they called, and all is well. It is not.

This is what really happens. You arrange to meet a friend at 11.00 am for coffee. You live some 30 minutes away but that's no big deal, you haven't seen the friend for some time. You arrive on time and wait. At 11.15 you receive a call from your 'mate',

'I am running late, be there soon!'

I know you're running late, its 11.15!!!

When you invite someone around for dinner, or suggest a get-together in the pub after work, have you noticed how frequently the response is;

'Let me check and I'll get back to you'.

This can be interpreted as

'Let me see if anything better comes up, otherwise I'll be there'.

This trend then extends into the situation where the invitation is accepted, followed by a cancellation closer to the time, something did come up.

What I'm getting at here is that if you have made plans keep to them. Treat appointments on a first come first serve basis. If you keep changing appointments the effect is a continual snowball effect. If your day happens to have four appointments scheduled, and the first one is delayed, do not delay all the others. Cut the first meeting short or reschedule it and then make sure all the others continue as planned. That way there is no time wasted. Not to mention that delaying people is extremely bad manners. Remember, they in turn may have sacrificed time and possibly other more pleasurable activities to make time to meet with you.

Be punctual, always

A logical extension to the previous paragraph, be punctual. And punctuality is not selective. Business or social appointments must be treated with the same cordiality of punctuality, as mentioned before you do not always know what sacrifices the other party has made.

Let me make a few suggestions. If someone has asked for an hour of your time, and arrived fifteen minutes late, give them 45 minutes only. If you are called to a meeting with someone, you arrive on time and are then kept waiting, leave. The message will soon be understood.

> *"It's difficult to prove yourself*
> *reliable when people are*
> *required to wait for you"*
>
> Wes Fesler

Being late is a bad habit, and some people I believe practice this for effect, what effect I'm not quite sure. Being late is bad manners, a complete waste of time which this is exactly what we are trying to avoid.

Take frequent breaks

It is not possible to operate at full power continuously for 8 hours. Every now and again it is a good idea to take a short break, which may be a walk to the coffee machine or just a minute's stretch looking out of the window. Exercise is an excellent way to relieve a tired mind, and many make use of fitness centres over lunch breaks.

As with most of what we have discussed here the implementation of these ideas must be practically considered and there will always be exceptions. For example, if we are doing something which requires complex thought and concentration and we happen to 'be on a roll' we would be reluctant to stop. In this case continue while the brain is hot, and only stop when that great period of concentration and productivity starts to fade.

Another idea is to stop what you're doing and do something else. Make a phone call, answer a letter, any change will provide relief.

A word of caution, you do not want this practice of short breaks to become what I refer to as the Coffee and Smoke break syndrome, discussed later in Chapter 14 – The Outside Factors

Match the time of day with tasks on hand

Everyone is different, some perform better in the early morning, others are unable to communicate intelligently and intelligibly before the sun is almost overhead. Try as one may I do not believe it is possible to change this innate behaviour, so the best you can do is to live with it and use it to your advantage.

Match your frame of mind to the tasks on hand. If you are a morning person, then use this time for something that requires the most brain power. When you are tired or during the 'bad' times of the day, address the more mundane tasks which although important will not require the same level of creativity and intelligence. Other people I know start to blossom when the sun sets, that's the time they should address their more challenging tasks.

Just a final point, if you find you are just not in the mood for the task, don't struggle, leave it for later and attend to something else.

Catch up in the morning, come in earlier

Notwithstanding what I mentioned above, one of the best times to catch up, and we all will fall behind at some time or other, is in the morning, early. One thing is for certain, the brain is fresher in the morning even if your own waking pattern takes longer than most. For whatever reason the early morning doesn't seem to take any time away from the rest of the day, and most of our leisure activities take place in the late afternoons and evenings.

Thus coming in early before the masses arrive and the phones start ringing allows an uninterrupted period to catch up on reading, and correspondence. To those of you who are just not morning people, you may have to find you own catch-up time.

Summary

Try these ideas. Although not always possible I am convinced there is merit in matching the task to the time of day. And ensure that you are, or become a punctual person, so much time is lost waiting for others, and The Longest Day wins.

12 - Some other tips and tricks

"People who multi-task do everything badly"

Anon

Here are a few little tricks you can employ to ensure you don't spend your evenings catching up, working late because of ridiculous schedules, unrealistic demands and expectations.

Do not accept more than you can do

There is nothing more stupid than accepting more than you are capable of handling. Please do not confuse this with a common business practice of unofficially accepting new work, even if at that point in time, there are insufficient resources to do the job. This practice is based on the likelihood that not all proposals for new business are accepted. It also follows that Airlines always overbook knowing that they will inevitably get no-shows.

What I'm talking about here is you. You are this one person, you only have two hands and already there is too much on your plate. If you know you absolutely cannot do something, then do not accept it.

I'm sure you're thinking,

'Yeah right, the boss comes along and says do this, and you say up yours daddy-o!'

Not quite, the art of saying no requires that you have an alternative.

If the boss comes along and asks for something to be completed by a certain deadline, request that the priorities of your existing workload are changed. One of the major reasons for advocating this approach is that if you have 6 tasks running concurrently, you can either do all of them nearly well, or 4 of them very well. There is another approach to a suggestion that if, for totally practical purposes, short cuts must be taken, drop a task completely, rather than doing all of them badly.

The psychological reaction to too much work must be considered. Once something is totally beyond one's reach there is no point in chasing the deadline. This inevitably leads to a total drop in productivity.

Multi-tasking is the art of screwing up everything at once.

Everyone has a limit to what they can achieve in a specific period. We must be able to multi-task but remember the cynical definition.

Do it right the first time

This old tried and tested cliché is still valid, and yet we continually bend or break this rule. Do not forget the conundrum to this is that we never have enough time to do it right the first time, and yet we always have time to fix it later.

It really is not difficult to do something correctly at the first pass. With careful planning and then making absolutely sure that the deliverable is understood by all

43

parties, getting it right is simple. The necessary preparation has been discussed above and I trust you are starting to see and understand the relevance of some of the earlier statements.

Choose when to experiment

Many of us like new gadgets and like to play with new toys. This is understandable and natural. Man's quest for information and innovation has led to the progress made to date. In addition if we did not experiment with new ideas we would not be able to improve, or expand or make the most out of emerging opportunities.

Having said that there is a time and a place for experimentation. I do not advocate the use of an important project to experiment with a new product or methodology. The learning curve associated with new ideas must not be underestimated and in addition many new toys may themselves be subject to unexpected difficulties. It would be advisable to experiment in a controlled non-critical environment before introducing throughout the corporation.

When you work, work

I have come in contact with many people from all walks of life, from all over the world. Many have told me that they always get to work early so that they have time to catch up on outstanding issues and be prepared for the day with a clean slate. This is something that I subscribe to, provided it's what actually happens when you get to work. What I have frequently noticed is that these early birds start the day by having coffee, scan the social media sites, check emails and then read the newspaper. If there are other early birds, they migrate towards one another and chat, more coffee and times goes by. By the time the 'official' workday starts they have not achieved anything.

If you understand this, and it's a way you like to start the day then well and good, provided you don't fool yourself.

Another real problem that so many of us suffer from is the ease with which we are interrupted, not by others but by our own thoughts, and indecision. The task is understood, but *'damn I haven't taken the dry-cleaning today'*. Or another urgent issue interrupts us. Then there are inevitable interruptions normally associated with open-plan offices and no-one can totally escape these. With practice it is possible to close your ears and mind to outside interferences.

Planning and a little self-discipline goes a long way to helping you focus and concentrate on the real issues. If you want to save time then when you work, make sure you work when it's time to do so.

Social media and phones significant interrupters and possibly the most difficult to ignore. Switch your phone off, social messages rarely require an instant response.

When you play, play

As a logical follow on from above, when it's time to stop work and relax or enjoy other activities then that is what you must do. Switch off.

Many people when on leave or just away for the weekend cannot avoid thinking about the office. Technology makes it so easy to 'let me answer this', a quick look at my messages and more. Leave your laptop or tablet at home, switch off your smart phone or better still, learn to ignore it.

Taking work on holiday totally defeats the objective of taking a break. I remember when going on holiday I would be uncontactable by any means for two or three weeks at a time. I made sure everything was up to date, someone was standing in for me and there was a delegated senior person to talk to should anything serious happen. This worked, no major problems, nobody died, and I returned refreshed.

It is extremely important to be able to switch off and allow the body and mind to recuperate. Hobbies and sport are excellent ways to relax, as the mind and body are required to work and concentrate on something entirely different.

Switching off may require practice, and a strong will. But remember that if you are relaxing you have chosen to do so. By default, that means that you have decided that work or other tasks will not be given attention.

There are I'm afraid a number of very irritating items that can severely test the relaxation process. The telephone and the mobile phone. I distinguish between the two as the telephone at home is easier to ignore, and of course if you're not at home no-one can get hold of you. The mobile phone is another story and appears to have taken control over everyone. The art of relaxation survival is to turn the damn thing off. If this is not practical, then you will have to learn that a "Sorry can't help now, I'm on leave" must be the standard response. Difficult I know but …

Remember that relaxing implies no worry as mentioned earlier. The two go together and the result of a good break is a refreshed body and mind. How you relax is your prerogative.

Manage upwards

Managing upwards is where you can influence your boss into making decisions which you firmly believe are better for you, your colleagues and the company. In the context of this book, you may want to influence a boss's behaviour which will in turn allow you to avoid The Longest Day.

There are several ways to do this.

Let the boss know how he or she will benefit from the changes you are proposing, not you. This will give your argument more credence. If the boss has a huge ego, then this approach has a better chance of success especially if you express your ideas subtly and don't mind if the boss takes the credit for them. (A good boss, if he or she agrees with your ideas, will give you the credit).

Timing is everything, if the boss is a morning person, that would be a good time. If there are major deadlines and the boss is under pressure, delay your approach.

Judge the boss's mood, and when you start your spiel, watch for signs of distraction. If you see or feel that boss is not really listening to you, suggest a meeting another time. I found that the best time to raise new ideas or concerns with the boss was to do so after hours, away from the office and in a social environment.

Whatever your issue is, present your case without emotion, certainly no anger nor aggression and once you have made your point, stop talking and wait for the response.

Be Honest

I have alluded to this in various parts of this book. People are loath to raise an alarm if they feel something is wrong, whistle blowers in UK companies seldom get the recognition and protection they deserve. Almost every report of something going wrong, a national computer system network failing, a building that floods because only later was it apparent that it was built on a flood plain. And the list goes on. I firmly believe that there is a common thread running through all these cases, staff knowing that there is a potential problem and not saying anything, or that the danger was identified but the decision makers decided to keep all under the carpet. Saying nothing knowing that something is very wrong, is no less 'criminal' that actively sabotaging a project.

In South Africa many years ago, there was a case where a company, looking to recruit a new employee, received a glowing reference from the previous employer. The candidate met all the job requirements and based on the reference was duly hired. It later became apparent that the person was not a superstar, and on investigation found that the reference from the previous employer was false. The previous employer was taken to court for providing false information.

Summary

In simple terms all we should be looking for is a balanced lifestyle. If you follow these simple guidelines you will be surprised at how so many problems and situations disappear and the rewards will look after themselves, goodbye Longest Day.

13 - The outside factors

"Control your own destiny or someone else will"

Jack Welch

The previous chapters discuss ideas and procedures that you should be able to control yourself. But as you are not alone in this world, there are many outside factors that will seriously test your ability to succeed.

There are many such influences that 'force' someone to waste time, and therefore introduce the need to catch up, and hence the long hours. There are other situations over which you will never have control and the sooner you learn to accept these and learn to live and work within theme the better.

If you recognise yourself in these scenarios and find that you enjoy these little distractions then you are either your own worst enemy, or you really don't want to work a normal day.

Office Canteens

Larger companies have canteens, and these are regarded as part of the employee benefits. Canteens reduce the need for staff to leave the premises for lunch and thus time is saved.

There is nothing wrong with this concept, but beware the trap of lingering, it wastes your time. I have certainly noticed those who start their day in the canteen, coffee, sandwiches, and that takes an hour. Then you'll notice them in the canteen for tea, then lunch and possibly in the evening. These are also the people who you will see spending longer hours in the office.

Quite simply it is possible to waste 2 to 3 hours a day in an office canteen and not even notice it. And don't immediately justify your behaviour by using business discussions as a reason. The intent may be there but in practice this is seldom a place for effective work communication.

Smoking areas

In the past smokers lit up wherever they wished and smoking in the office at the work place was common. With the emphasis on health and the protection of one group from the bad practices of another, smoking in all buildings and public places is now banned. This has led to groups of people appearing outside the office, on the pavements, having their quick smoke.

This practice wasted hours a day, which for the conscientious meant having to stay late to complete the day's work. Fortunately this is becoming less and less of a problem.

Labour laws

The international trend of being politically correct has severely restricted a company's ability to advertise and employ the right person for a specific job. We are no longer allowed to mention race, sex or age, and yet these may be fundamental to the nature of the job on hand. Furthermore, there are countries whose laws insist that the make-up of the work force follows the demographics of the country, irrespective of qualifications of the candidates. Labour laws also limit the number of hours per day people can work, boy does this force clock watching!

Freedom of speech and political correctness

Freedom of speech and political correctness contradict each other. You have the right to state your mind and yet are castigated for being specific. We now have to soften the definition and/or description of a person, condition, appearance and so on the point of being misleading at best or downright incorrect at worst.

A UK recruiter was stunned when her advert for 'reliable' and 'hard-working applicants was rejected by the job centre as it could be offensive to unreliable and lazy people

One of the most damaging of traits is that unwillingness to tell the truth for fear of upsetting someone.

Someone knew about those activities but neglected to report them. A prime example of this relates to Pakistani gangs abusing 1,400 Rotherham children. The police forces lean over backwards to avoid the accusation of racism, while social workers will hesitate to intervene in any case in which they could be accused of discriminating against ethnic minorities.

We British are masters of this trait, have you noticed that if you voice your opinion to someone and they don't share your view, they just say nothing and walk away! Quite simply political correctness forces one to avoid the truth.

Empowerment

Management by committee, empowering everyone to focus on their own agendas wastes a lot of time. Certainly it is worthwhile to listen to people's views, however there still is a need for a single decision maker, a point made earlier in this book.

People affected by any decisions like to be part of the decision-making process or at least have their say, and if this is done correctly the likelihood of staff support is increased. Military style management in the office environment has seen little success. But be careful, try to stem the discussions, and ensure the objectives are not forgotten.

There was a superb comment in a movie, where an Army officer was faced with an irate junior who felt that the orders could not be followed as others had not been counselled, to which the Senior officer replied,

"Political correctness is a doctrine fostered by a delusional, illogical minority, and rapidly promoted by mainstream media, which holds forth the proposition that it's entirely possible to pick up a piece of shit by the clean end"
ANON

"We're here to defend democracy, not to practice it"

Office location

The office location, wherever it is will have both positives and negatives. This is a double-edged sword.

I have advocated taking short breaks, and in this regard, it is nice to be able to leave the office and take a lunchtime stroll around the shopping mall or browse in a book store. Exercise is good, and the brain is given a well-earned rest. To enable this the office location needs to be close to the amenities I've just mentioned.

Many large corporations tend to place their business premises away from the down town areas, and thus anyone wishing to do odd chores over lunchtime would have to drive or take public transport. These corporations invariably have their own canteens, have fitness gyms and classes understanding that once you arrive at work you're there for the day. I believe it is important to take breaks and feel that remote office locations can be detrimental in this regard.

Health and Safety

The increase in the safety-first culture is quite frightening. What was once common sense has now become an industry of small-minded people looking for every conceivable way to avoid an accident and failing that, having someone else to blame for their demise.

Every product must have warnings which are, in almost all cases totally ridiculous.

'This blade is likely to be very sharp'

'Peanut butter 'may contain nuts''

Sign on a hot tap *'beware of hot water'* and so it goes on.

You see TV presenters wearing life jackets in ankle deep water.

The word accident has all but been removed from the dictionary and is longer an acceptable reason for an occurrence and it is always someone else's fault.

"The reason I am fat is because of MacDonald's hamburgers".

The fact that the individual ate 14 a day doesn't enter the discussion.

> *"If we accept that there is no such thing as 'zero' risk then we should not spin the meaning of words with assertions such as 'all accidents' are preventable"*
>
> **Dr Rob Long**

You can tell that this subject annoys me intensely, but there are far more significant implications. Almost everything you do these days whether at work or privately is affected by this 'protective' culture. There are many businesses out there specialising in providing mandatory training for subjects such as, how to use scissors, how to climb a ladder, how to rescue people in ankle deep water and so on. This adds time and cost to almost every product and service we make use of.

Health and Safety makes life very difficult for a forward thinking, adventurous and pioneering person who only wants to do a better job.

What is very concerning, is the high number of people in the UK who have stress related disorders, the figure is something like one in four. I wonder if this phenomenon is caused by the fact that people are continually being warned of the dangers of anything and everything, the weather, food, walking, running, team sports, electricity, hot water, cold water and being alive.

No wonder the current generation is called the 'snowflake generation'.

Peer pressure

Some of your biggest obstacles will be your peers and not all your peers are going to be friends. All people to a greater or lesser extent suffer from the "RTC" (*Resistance to Change)* factor. The corporate environment is competitive, and these non-friends will seize any opportunity they can to belittle your new approach and use it to their own advantage. We also mentioned earlier that those around you who are the long-hours advocates will become defensive of their own practices and be suspicious of your motives.

Those who are your friends will obviously support you but even here you will need to explain your motives and objectives very clearly. Winning people over requires that they understand from where you are coming.

Company Culture

You will find it very difficult to fight the inbred culture of a large organisation. Every company has its own style and personality, this is seldom written down nor is it intentional. The culture is brought about by the personalities of the management and staff they employ, and this is very difficult to change. Those who have tried for reasons of necessity have found such a change can take a generation to achieve.

"Insanity: doing the same thing over and over again and expecting the same result"

Albert Einstein

This is not to say that you cannot achieve your own goals within such an organisation, but it can be very difficult. It is important that you understand this challenge. Many people have found that implementing a personal change is best done in a new environment and if you feel you cannot achieve your own personal goals for this reason, it may be optimal to move.

Personal Culture

People from different cultures and backgrounds react differently in certain situations. The one that causes the most trouble is those who are afraid of be forthright when questioned about, anything.

When asked for an opinion on something they say what they think the questioner wants to hear, or what will least offend. You are probably familiar with the question

'Does my bum look big in these jeans'?

In business this is far more serious. Frequently staff have been afraid to raise the alarm about pending problems, they keep quiet, knowing that;

'this won't work for these reasons', or

'that hasn't been done yet, I am incapable of performing that task.'.

If anything can force long hours this attitude will.

"Even if you're on the right track, you'll get run over if you just sit there"

Will Rogers

If you are asked to review a hotel, or restaurant or company, do you tell them the truth, I hope so. Companies can go bust if you don't.

As I said in the beginning of this chapter there are some things over which you have no control. What you need to do is to identify these aspects that affect you, understand the effect and then work out in your own mind how important they are to your well-being. Then either accept them or adapt accordingly.

Summary

Many of the above provide one with a more interesting and diverse working and living environment, this is positive. The difficulties come when people are unable to come to terms with aspects of work and life that don't suit them. But there comes a time when you will not beat these influences so its best get on with it or stay out of the kitchen.

But whatever we feel we don't want to add to our challenges by adopting The Longest Day.

14 - How to practice the above

"If you don't like something, change it. If you can't change it, change your attitude. Don't complain."

Maya Angelou

As is always the case with theory versus practical, changing your approach will not be easy, mainly as there are many factors which directly or indirectly will disturb your well-intentioned approach. However, if you have taken the decision to change, like a New Year resolution which may be to stop smoking or lose weight, then you must persevere.

The challenge is to follow these guidelines and become your own person. Firstly, many of the suggestions can be applied to a non-work environment, start by introducing your new ideas into your social life. This will afford you the opportunity of practising amongst friends,

If you then want to put these ideas into practice at work then go ahead, but tread carefully, especially if you suspect your peers, superiors or the whole company may have difficulty accepting your new ideas. I do not suggest you make a public announcement to all concerned that from tomorrow you will only work 8 hours a day! That's looking for trouble. A better approach would be to start practising these points with your friends in your social circle. They will soon tell you if you're on the right track or off your rocker.

Then take things one step at a time. As soon as you are able, elicit the help and support from a colleague, a partner in this will be a great advantage.

We discussed the many outside factors which will have an impact on your mission. Consider these carefully and ensure that you understand which will affect you and to what extent.

Then there are the customers who, notwithstanding some of the things I said earlier, dictate to a large extent how we are able to function. This is not to say that you cannot implement new ideas, but you will have to be flexible from time to time.

One of the best ways of achieving a change, when it requires that those around you understand and accept another concept or approach, is to explain the rationale behind your thinking.

'I thought that if I changed the design we could save time by doing it this way, and the result would be more accurate'.

If faced with an instruction that may invoke a negative response, don't just say no, explain the reason and then offer an alternative.

'I cannot do it now, but I can do it then'.

Your alternative is positive, and you'll win friends that way.

To summarise:

- identify the outside factors which are likely to affect your scenario the most
- decide on what you cannot change, and then decide on how you are going to live with this
- start with the changes that you feel are the easiest to implement
- get yourself an ally as soon as possible
- implement the changes one at a time
- do not announce your plans to all
- when you have succeeded in one area, move on to the next.

Finally set yourself reasonable deadlines. If you try to achieve too much too soon, you will place yourself under undue pressure and this we have covered already.

At this stage you are well on the way to avoiding The Longest Day.

PART FOUR – CONCLUSION

"I cannot say whether things will get better if we change; what I can say is they must change if they are to get better"

G.C. Lichtenberg

Anð now it is all up to you. As I have mentioned more than once, it is not easy to suddenly change your approach to both work and social life. Don't try and do everything at once, ease into the changes that you wish to make.

Any changes will require a certain amount of self-discipline and from that the 'new' approach must ultimately become a habit, such as the ability to say no.

What many may find difficult is the ability to understand when the new rules must be broken. As with all theories and good ideas, the absolute success is knowing when to enforce your beliefs and when not to.

Notwithstanding anything in this book, you must do what works for you. If you enjoy doing all your email on Saturday morning, then do it. Just remember that long hours do not relate to productivity.

Much of what has been said relies on having the right people, and probably enough resources to do everything. There will never be enough, and this is yet another reason to work smart, which means spend less time on tasks without compromising the product.

You may find that everything you try and do is in total conflict with the company's culture. If that is the case, then I'm sorry, take it or leave. There is no sense in embarking on a mission that has zero chance of success.

You may not be able to introduce everything you would like, but some of the ideas you will find can make a tremendous difference to you and will not necessarily upset those around you. It is still worth trying some of these changes, every bit can give you a life.

How does one eat an elephant?

One bite at a time!

Inevitably, some readers will come back to me and say that, for these reasons, this will not work under these circumstances. When this happens I am likely to respond,

'Do not tell me why it won't work, tell me why it will!'

From here on in the rest is up to you, if you try some of these ideas and you really want to start having a life, go for it.

If not, you will always be one of those who works

The Longest Day.

APPENDIX

About the Author

Jeremy Tindall was born in South Africa in 1949, attended school at Kearsney College where he obtained a first class matric in 1966. He has B.Comm. degree majoring in Economics and Business Economics from the University of South Africa.

He spent most of his working life in the computer industry working in South Africa, Europe, and the middle and far east. Starting his career as a computer programmer he progressed into systems analysis, project management and company management. He established himself as an independent business and strategy consultant working internationally.

A very keen sportsman and scuba diver his first book, *An Underwater guide to Coral Fishes of the Indian Ocean*, published in 1991.

How to avoid The Longest Day is a far cry from the oceans. Based on a culmination of his experiences in the IT world and business consulting across many industries, the book examines those who spend long hours working at the office, highlights the negatives pertaining to this practice and provides practical advice on how to minimise long hours and increase productivity.

Terminology used

Deliverable

This is the end result of the project, is you are building a boat, the boat is the deliverable if you are providing a service like consulting then the advice provided is the deliverable.

Project

For the purposes of clarity and consistency I used the term 'project' to describe any job or chore or task that has to be performed. A project has a start date, any number of sub-tasks and a completion. In all cases projects will have requirements, desired results and only once these requirements have been met can the project be deemed as complete.

Requirements

Before starting any task, one has in mind a picture of the desired result. If you are sewing, you know what the end article should like, its size and colour. If you're building a house the same applies. If you are designing something you decide what you want and how it should look and perform. Hence you know the requirements of the task before you start, or you should as will be apparent later.